The Voice Of The Silence

Yogi Ramacharaka

Because this article has been extracted from a parent book, it may have non-pertinent text at the beginning or end of it.

Any blank pages following the article are necessary for our book production requirements. The article herein is complete.

LESSON IV.

THE VOICE OF THE SILENCE.

Part II of *"Light on the Path"* opens with the following statement:

Out of the silence that is peace, a resonant voice shall arise. And this voice will say: It is not well, thou has reaped, now thou must sow. And, knowing this voice to be the silence itself, thou wilt obey.

The resonant voice that proceeds from "out of the silence that is peace" is the voice of Spirit forcing its way into the field of consciousness. The voice is not as plain as when heard at the moment of illumination, for the ear is filled with the vibrations of the lower planes, and cannot sense so clearly the high vibrations proceeding from the upper regions of the mind. But the voice is insistent, and if listened to will make itself heard. It will not be confused with the thought-waves with which the ether is filled. for when one thinks of the spiritual plane he is lifted upward mentally, and the lower vibrations cannot reach him so plainly. He soon learns to distinguish the clear pure voice of Spirit from the grosser thought-waves that are beating upon him. The voice of Spirit always has an "upward" tendency, and its influence is always toward higher things.

"And this voice will say: It is not well; thou hast reaped, now thou must sow." This passage pictures the longing which possesses the true occultist, who has experienced the higher consciousness, and which

impels him to carry out in actual life the truth which
he has received—to manifest in action and associa-
tion with the world, the thought which has come to
him in the silence.

The soul may wait in solitude until the truth comes
to it—but the truth, when once received and given a
lodgment in the heart, fills the soul with a divine
unrest, and causes it to go forth into the world and
live the life of the Spirit among and with men, in-
stead of apart and away from them. The man to
whom spiritual illumination has come—even in its
lightest form—is a changed being. He radiates
thought of a different character from that emanat-
ing from the minds of those around him. He has
different ideals and consequently different thoughts.
And his thought-waves have an effect upon the great
body of thought-waves of the world. They leaven
the mass—they are like the stream of pure water
pouring into the muddy pond, which pure stream
gradually clears the entire pond. His thoughts and
presence are needed in the world's work, and so the
Spiritual Mind sends him an impulse to go forth and
live the life—to live it among men and women, and
not apart from them. It says to him: "Thou hast
reaped, now thou must sow." "And knowing this
voice to be the silence itself," he obeys.

There are three great stages in the spiritual and
mental life of the race, and as the babe before birth
goes through all the physical changes, shapes and
forms that the race has passed through during long
ages of evolution, so does the growing man go through

the stages of the mental and spiritual evolution of the race.   But the individual goes through only such changes as lead up to the stage of evolution he has reached at full maturity.   He may reach only Stage I, if he is a Stage I individual.   If he is a Stage II individual he passes through Stage I and then on to Stage II.   If he is a Stage III soul, he passes through Stage I, and then Stage II (as rapidly as may be) and then unfolds into the Stage III consciousness.   Let us consider these three stages.

Stage I is that plane of life in which the Instinctive Mind is in control, the Intellect not being sufficiently developed to assert itself fully and the Spiritual Mind being scarcely recognized.   In this stage live the primitive races—and the young child.   Those dwelling in it have but little concern for aught but that which pertains to the physical life.   Their thoughts are mainly those relating to food, shelter, and the gratification of the physical senses.   There exists among these people a certain freedom, democracy, and a lack of the "I am holier than thou" or "better than thou" feeling, which renders their life freer and easier, and happier, than that of those in the next highest stage.   They know little or nothing about "sin," and generally follow their desires without question.   They have a sort of instinctive belief in a higher power, but do not trouble themselves much about it, nor do they imagine that certain ceremonies or observances are pleasing to Deity, and that failure to perform are apt to arouse his wrath.   They do not worry much about their chances of "salvation," and are disposed instinc-

tively to realize that the Power that takes care of them
Here, will take care of them There.

Stage II commences when the Intellect begins to as-
sume control. Man then begins to awaken to a sense
of "good and evil." He recognizes a mysterious something coming from a still higher part of his mind,
which makes him feel ashamed of doing certain selfish
things, and which causes him to experience a feeling
of peace and satisfaction when he has done certain
(comparatively) unselfish things. But the Intellect
does not stop with this. It begins to invent "good"
things, and "bad" things. Priests and prophets arise
who say that certain things (usually the giving of a
part of one's goods to the temple) are "good" and
pleasing to Deity; and that certain other things (for
instance, the refusal to attend the temple, or to con-
tribute to its support) are "bad" and certain to be punished by Deity. These priests and prophets invent
heavens suited to the desires of their followers, and
hells filled with the particular things that their people
fear. Things are separated into "good" and "bad,"
the "bad" list seeming to be the larger. Most of the
pleasant things of life are placed in the "bad" list for
no other reason than that they *are* pleasant. In the
same way the "good" list includes the majority of
unpleasant things, the prevailing idea being that
Deity delights in seeing his children doing things unpleasant to them, and waxes wroth if they chance to
indulge in a pleasant act. Creeds and sects are de-
vised, and dire punishment is meted to those who do

not accept the former and join the latter. The idea seems to be that those who do not agree with one's particular conception of Deity are "against God," or "God's enemies," and must and will be punished by him. People often prefer to relieve God of the task of punishing these unbelievers, and proceed to do it themselves.

People in this stage of spiritual development are usually quite strenuous. They declare certain days to be "holy" (as if all days were not so) and insist that certain places are holier than' others. They claim that certain peoples and races are "chosen" and favored, and that the rest are hated by Deity. They insist that only a handful of men are to be "saved," and that the majority of God's children are destined to everlasting damnation and punishment. Hell is very hot when seen from the viewpoint of Stage II. Hate, arising from the feeling of self-righteousness, is a marked characteristic of this stage—sects are formed, and hate and jealousy are manifested between them. Fear reigns, and the Divine Love is almost lost sight of. The Brotherhood of Man is but a name in this stage—all the brotherly feeling that is to be seen is confined to the people belonging to some particular sect. The outsiders are not "brothers," but "heathen," "pagans," "unbelievers," "dissenters," "heretics," etc. The sense of the Oneness of All, which is instinctively felt in Stage I (and both seen and felt in Stage III), is apparently neither seen or felt in Stage II. In this stage separateness seems to be the keynote. As the race passes still further along in this stage, and In-

tellect further unfolds, the reasoning faculties cause
it to discard many superstitions and foolish notions
that had at one time seemed sacred and the truth itself.
Sheath after sheath is discarded as outworn and no
longer necessary, and usually a period of disbelief and
skepticism sets in. The old things have been thrown
aside, but nothing seems to have come to take their
place. But after this phase, the Spiritual Mind seems
to concentrate its effort to force into the field of consciousness the internal evidence of the truth—of real
religion—of the teachings of Spirit. And Man gradually passes into Stage III.

Stage III people see good in everyone—in all things
—in every place. Some things are seen to be more
highly developed than others, but all are seen to form
a part of the great plan. The developed soul parts
with certain things from lack of desire, casting them
off as worn out tools or clothing. But it sees that
to others these same things are the best they have,
and are far better than some other things which these
undeveloped people had parted company with still
farther back. It sees that all of life is on the Path—
some a little farther advanced than others, but all
journeying in the same direction. It sees all learning their lessons and profiting by their mistakes. It
sees manifestations of both "good" and "bad" (relative terms) in each man and woman, but prefers to
look for the "good" in the sinner, rather than for
the "bad" in the saint. It sees in "sin" principally
mistakes, misdirected energy, and undeveloped mind.

The Stage III soul sees good in all forms of religions—so much so that it finds it hard to follow the narrow creeds of any particular one. It sees the Absolute worshiped and recognized in all the conceptions of Deity that have ever originated in the human mind, from the stone idol to the highest conception of Deity known to any of "the churches," the difference being solely in the spiritual growth of the different worshipers. As man grows, his *conception* of Deity advances—a man's idea of God is merely himself magnified. The God of the advanced man does not appeal to the savage, any more than does the God of the savage attract the advanced man. Each is doing the best he can, and is setting up a conception corresponding to his particular stage of growth. A writer has aptly expressed this thought in these words: "A man's god is himself at his best, and his devil is himself at his worst." But devils pass away from Man as his conception of Deity enlarges.

But the great distinguishing thought of the Stage III man is his consciousness of the Oneness of All. He sees, and feels, that all the world is alive and full of intelligence in varying degrees of manifestation. He feels himself a part of that great life. He feels his identity with all of Life. He feels in touch with all of nature—in all its forms. In all forms of life he sees something of himself, and recognizes that each particular form of life has its correspondence in something within himself. This does not mean that he is blood-thirsty like the tiger; vain like the peacock; venomous like the serpent. But, still he feels that all the attributes of these animals are within

himself—mastered and governed by his higher self—
but still there.   And consequently he can feel for
these animals, or for those of his race in which the
animal characteristics are still in evidence. He pities
them, but does not hate his brother however much
that brother's traits may seem undesirable and hurtful
to him. And he feels within himself all the attributes
of the higher life as well as the lower, and he realizes
that he is unfolding and growing into these higher
forms, and that some day he will be like them.

He feels the great throbbing life of which he is a
part—and he feels it to be *his* life. The sense of separateness is slipping from him. He feels the security
that comes from this consciousness of his identity with
the All Life, and consequently he cannot Fear. He
faces to-day and to-morrow without fear, and marches
forward toward the Divine Adventure with joy in
his heart. He feels at home, for is not the Universe
akin to him—is he not among his own?

Such a consciousness divests one of Fear, and Hate,
and Condemnation. It teaches one to be kind.   It
makes one realize the Fatherhood of God and the
Brotherhood of Man. It substitutes a *knowing* for a
blind belief. It makes man over, and starts him on
a new stage of his journey, a changed being.

No wonder that one in this Stage III is misunderstood by Stage II people. No wonder that they often
consider him to be a Stage I man because he fails
to see "evil" in what seems so to them. No wonder
that they marvel at his seeing "good" in things that
do not appear so to them. He is like a stranger in a

strange land, and must not complain if he be misjudged and misunderstood. But there are more and more of these people every year—they are coming in great quantities, and when they reach a sufficient number, this old earth will undergo a peaceful revolution. In that day man no longer will be content to enjoy luxury while his brother starves—he will not be able to oppress and exploit his own kind—he will not be able to endure much that to-day is passed over without thought and feeling by the majority of people And why will he not be able to do these things? may be asked by some. Simply because the man who has experienced this new consciousness has broken down the old feeling of separateness, and his brother's pain is felt by him—his brother's joy is experienced by him—he is in touch with others.

From whence comes this uneasiness that causes men to erect hospitals, and other charitable institutions—from whence comes this feeling of discomfort at the sight of suffering? From the Spiritual Mind that is causing the feeling of nearness to all of life to awaken in the mind of man, and thus renders it more and more painful for them to see and be aware of the pain of others—because they begin to *feel* it, and it renders them uncomfortable, and they make at least some effort to relieve it. The world is growing kinder by reason of this dawning consciousness, although it is still in a barbarous state as compared to its future condition when Stage III becomes more common. The race to-day confronts great changes—the thousand straws floating through the air show from which direction the wind is coming, and whither it is blowing. The breeze is just beginning to be felt—soon it will grow stronger, and then the gale will come which will sweep before it much that man has thought to be built for ages. And after the storm man will build better things—things that will endure. Have you not noticed the signs—have you not felt the breeze? But, mark you this—the final change will come not from Hate, Revenge, or other unworthy motives—it will come as the result of a great and growing Love —a feeling that will convince men that they are akin; that the hurt of one is the hurt of all; that the joy of one is the joy of all—that all are One. Thus will come the dawn of the Golden Age.

We may have appeared to have wandered from our text, but what we have said has a direct bearing upon the question of sowing after the reaping—of giving after the receiving—of working after the acquiring of new strength. The voice out of the silence will indeed say to all of us: Go forth and labor in my vineyard—labor not by strenuous effort, or by an attempt to force the growth of living things—thy work is best done by *living*—you are needed as leaven to lighten the mass.

Here follows the next command from the little manual:

Thou who are now a disciple, able to stand, able to hear, able to see, able to speak; who hast conquered desire, and attained to self-knowledge; who hast seen thy soul in its bloom, and recognized it, and heard the voice of the silence —go thou to the Hall of Learning, and read what is written there for thee.

Let us also read the note following this command;
it is very helpful:

NOTE.—To be able to stand, is to have confidence; to be
able to hear, is to have opened the doors of the soul; to
be able to see, is to have obtained perception; to be able to
speak, is to have attained the power of helping others; to
have conquered desire, is to have learned how to use and
control the self; to have attained to self-knowledge, is to
have retreated to the inner fortress from whence the personal
man can be viewed with impartiality; to have seen thy soul
in its bloom, is to have obtained a momentary glimpse in
thyself of the transfiguration which shall eventually make
thee more than man; to recognize, is to achieve the great
task of gazing upon the blazing light without dropping the
eyes, and not falling back in terror as though before some
ghastly phantom. This happens to some; and so, when the
victory is all but won, it is lost. To hear the voice of silence,
is to understand that from within comes the only true guidance; to go to the Hall of Learning, is to enter the state in
which learning becomes possible. Then will many words be
written there for thee, and written in fiery letters for thee
easily to read. For, when the disciple is ready, the Master
is ready also.

The disciple is spoken of as one able to stand; able
to hear; able to see; able to speak. The consciousness of the Real Self enables one to stand firmly upon
his feet—causes him to feel the Majesty of Self. It
enables him to hear the truth pouring in to him from
the thousand channels of life, all claiming kinship
with him, and willing and anxious to impart to him
knowledge and truth. It enables him to see life as
it is, in all its varied forms—to see his relation to
the Whole and all of its parts, and to recognize the
truth when it presents itself before him—it gives him
the clear vision of the Spirit. It enables him to speak
so that his words will reach others, even when he is
unconscious of the fact—he is possessed of that peace
which passeth understanding, and his inward state

finds utterance in his everyday speech, and he adds a little to the spiritual knowledge of the world.

The manual tells the student who has conquered desire—that is, who has recognized desire for what it is, who has attained to the knowledge of the Self; who has seen his soul in its bloom, and recognized it, and heard the voice of the silence; to proceed to the Hall of Learning, and read what is written there for him. The little note throws additional light on the passage which it follows. Its description of the sight of "the soul in its bloom" is particularly interesting in view of what we have said in our last lesson—it refers to Illumination, or the dawn of spiritual consciousness—the flower that blooms in the silence that follows the storm. Well does its writer say that it is "to have obtained a momentary glimpse in thyself of the transfiguration which shall eventually make thee more than man; to recognize is to achieve the great task of gazing upon the blazing light without dropping the eyes, and not falling back in terror as though before some ghastly phantom." Well has the writer added that "This happens to some; and so when the victory is all but won, it is lost." But she might have added, that it is only temporarily lost, for the memory will remain, and the soul will never rest satisfied until it regains that which it lost. Some who catch glimpses of their souls, shrink back in fright, and treat the matter as a delusion, or some "wicked thought." It upsets one's preconceived and conventional notions to such a degree, in some instances, that those experiencing it begin to be afraid that they are losing their virtue and goodness, because they cease to condemn and hate "evil" as of yore—they imagine that they are growing "bad," and retreat from the consciousness so far as they are able. They fail to perceive that although one may hate the "bad" things less, he loves the "good" things more than ever—that is the things which are known to be good by the Spiritual Mind, not the manufactured and artificial "good" things that pass current as the real article with the majority of people.

The little note also truthfully tells us that "To hear the voice of the silence is to understand that from within comes the only true guidance." Remember these words—they are golden: *"Understand that from within comes the only true guidance."* If you can grasp the meaning of these words—and have the courage to trust and believe them, you are well started on the Path. If you will always live true to that little voice within, there will be but little need of teachers and preachers for you. And if we will but trust that little voice, its tones will become plainer and stronger, and we will hear it on many occasions. But if we turn a deaf ear to it and refuse to heed its warning and guidance, it will gradually grow fainter and fainter, until its voice is no longer distinguishable amidst the roar and bustle of the material world.

The Hall of Learning is the state of consciousness which comes when the Spiritual Mind is allowed to flow freely into the conscious mind. Little by little the student is impressed with the truth, so gradually, often, that he scarcely realizes that it is advancing—but he is continually progressing and unfolding.

The next four precepts are very important. Although intended for quite advanced students, much of
their meaning may be grasped by those who have not
attained so fully. We will try to make a little plainer
these difficult passages.

1. Stand aside in the coming battle; and, though thou
fightest, be not thou the warrior.

2. Look for the warrior, and let him fight in thee.

3. Take his orders for battle, and obey them.

4. Obey him, not as though he were a general, but as
though he were thyself, and his spoken words were the utterance of thy secret desires; for he is thyself, yet infinitely
wiser and stronger than thyself. Look for him, else, in
the fever and hurry of the fight, thou mayest pass him;
and he will not know thee unless thou knowest him. If thy
cry reach his listening ear, then will he fight in thee, and
fill the dull void within. And, if this is so, then canst thou
go through the fight cool and unwearied, standing aside, and
letting him battle for thee. Then it will be impossible for
thee to strike one blow amiss. But if thou look not for him,
if thou pass him by, then there is no safeguard for thee.
Thy brain will reel, thy heart grow uncertain, and, in the
dust of the battle-field, thy sight and senses will fail, and
thou wilt not know thy friends from thy enemies.

He is thyself; yet thou are but finite, and liable to error.
He is eternal, and is sure. He is eternal truth. When once
he has entered thee, and become thy warrior, he will never
utterly desert thee; and, at the day of the great peace, he
will become one with thee.

These four precepts refer to the recognition of the
Real Self—Spirit—which is within each soul, and
which is constantly struggling to cast from itself (when
the time is ripe) each encumbering sheath of the lower
self which is hindering and confining it. The precepts
bid the soul to look within for the real source of
strength—to be guided by it—to allow it to manifest
freely through oneself—to be led by Spirit. When one
has sufficiently freed oneself from the restrictions and
confining bonds of the lower self, and is able to allow

Spirit to flow freely and manifest with a minimum degree of resistance, then will Spirit act through him and work for him, and guide him.   And even the less advanced soul may obtain the greatest benefit from opening up itself to the inflow of the divine principle, and allowing it to work through it.   The man who is led by Spirit—who recognizes the existence of the Real Self, and trusts it—may live in a great measure apart from the turmoil and strife of the outer world. Not that he may withdraw from the world (for that is often cowardice), but he is able to take his place in the great game of Life, and to do his work there and do it well, and yet feel certain that while he is *in* it he is not *of* it.   He is able practically to stand aside and see himself act.   Spirit will guide him through the struggle, and will see that he is nourished and cared for, and will always act for his *ultimate* good. It will lead him to that which is best for him, and will attract to him that which he needs.   Fear and unfaith are the great obstacles to this free working of Spirit, and until they are cast aside Spirit is hampered and hindered in its work.   But when they are thrown aside Spirit will be free to do its work.

The first precept: "Stand aside in the coming battle; and though thou fightest, be thou not the warrior," states this truth distinctly.   Note that the precept does not tell you to run away from the battle, or to hide yourself, or to seek seclusion.   On the contrary, it distinctly assumes that you will fight.   But it tells you to "stand aside" (that is for you, in your present consciousness to stand aside) and let the real self fight through you and for you. That is, to allow Spirit to lead you, and for you to be content with its leading.

The second precept is akin to the first. It tells you to "Look for the warrior, and let him fight in thee." Look for him; believe in him; trust in him; recognize him—and let him fight the battle for you.

"Take his orders for battle, and obey them," says the third precept. If he places you in a certain exposed position, where the enemy's fire is concentrated upon you, and your retreat seems to be utterly cut off, fear not but obey orders implicitly, for there is a plan behind the orders, and you will in the end triumph. Question not the orders, nor their result, for they are given by a higher form of intelligence than your present consciousness, and have a distinct (and good) object in view. Spirit is moving for your advancement, and though it brings you temporary pain and suffering, you will be a gainer in the end. And if you once grasp the meaning of it all, you will not feel the suffering and the pain as do others, for they will be seen to be only temporary and fleeting, and unreal, and you will lose sense of them in your knowledge of the greater thing coming to you through and by means of them.

The fourth precept tells you further to "Obey him, not as though he were a general, but as though he were thyself, and his spoken words were the utterance of thy secret desires; for he is thyself, yet infinitely wiser and stronger than thyself." This admonition serves to warn us of the mistake of considering Spirit as an outside entity—a thing apart

from ourself—and to remind us that it is our *real* self
—*ourself*. Wiser and stronger than our present conception and consciousness of self, is Spirit, and we
may trust it implicitly.

"Look for him, else, in the fever and hurry of the
fight, thou mayest pass him; and he will not know
thee unless thou knowest him," continues the precept, and the warning is worthy of note. In the midst
of the fight we are most apt to forget that the Real
Self is working through us, and, being excited and
inflated by success, we may imagine that *we* (the conscious self) are doing all the work, and may cease
to look for the Spirit, and thus close the channel of
communication. "And he will not know thee, unless
thou knowest him." Unless you recognize Spirit
within, Spirit will not be able to work through you as
freely as would otherwise be the case. Unless you
recognize the existence of Spirit, you cannot expect
it to respond. Spirit's guidance is for those who desire it and look for it.

"If thy cry reach his listening ear, then will he
fight in thee, and fill the dull void within." Note
the promise, and the statement that Spirit is listening
—ever listening—for your call for help. When you
become disheartened and discouraged—tired and worn
from the fight—wounded and bleeding from the struggle—then cry to Spirit for help, and the listening ear
will hear thee and will "fight in thee and fill the dull
void within." He who opens himself up to Spirit no
longer is conscious of the "dull void within" which
has oppressed him for so long.

"And if this is so, then canst thou go through the fight and unwearied, standing aside, and letting him battle for thee." You will gain that feeling of calm content, knowing that thy warrior is invincible, and that the battle must be yours in the end. He who is conscious of Spirit working through him has indeed acquired "that peace which passeth understanding."

"Then it will be impossible for thee to strike one blow amiss." True, indeed, for then every act and move is the act and movement of Spirit, and cannot be amiss or wrong. No matter how meaningless or mistaken the act or move may seem to the conscious mind, at the time, later on it will be recognized as having been the very best thing under the circumstances.

"But if thou look not for him, if thou pass him by, then there is no safeguard for thee. Thy brain will reel, thy heart grow uncertain, and, in the dust of the battle-field, thy sight and senses will fail, and thou will not know thy friends from thy enemies." Is not this the experience of all of us before we recognize and trust Spirit's guidance? Have we not gone through these things, and suffered and grieved because we could see no light; no hope? Long have we cried aloud, demanding to know the reason of it all—demanding to be told what was truth; what was right; what was wrong. And no answer has come to us, until we threw off the confining bonds of the lower self, and allowed the pure rays of Spirit to pour into our souls.

"He is thyself; yet thou are but finite, and liable to error. He is eternal, and is sure. He is eternal truth." The distinction between the lower, temporary, consciousness of self, and the reality, is here pointed out. The paradox of the self and the Self is here presented to you. Think well over it, and the truth will gradually reach you—and having reached you will never again depart from you, no matter how dim it may seem at times.

"When once he has entered thee, and become thy warrior, he will never utterly desert thee." Wonderful promise. The consciousness of the existence of the Spirit within you, once obtained, is never entirely lost. Though you may learn to doubt it, as not having come through your ordinary senses, yet will the memory linger with you—and when it is most needed you will be able to recall the experience and again open yourself to the inflow of the divine wisdom and power.

"And, at the day of the great peace, he will become one with thee." In the time when sheath after sheath has been cast off and the flower of Spirit unfolds in full bloom—when man shall become more than man—then will the consciousness of the individual melt into the "knowing" of Spirit, and the soul will be at one with its highest principle. This will not be a surrender of individuality—but, on the contrary will be such an enlargement of individuality and consciousness as can scarcely be imagined by the greatest intellect of to-day. Then the great knowing, power, and joy, of which we have gained a faint glimpse during the flash of illumination, will become a permanent consciousness with us. Then will we pass from the realms of the relative into the regions of the absolute.

We come now to another group of four precepts. Let us consider them.

5. Listen to the song of life.
6. Store in your memory the melody you hear.
7. Learn from it the lesson of harmony.
8. You can stand upright now, firm as a rock amid the turmoil, obeying the warrior who is thyself and thy king. Unconcerned in the battle save to do his bidding, having no longer any care as to the result of the battle—for one thing only is important, that the warrior shall win; and you know he is incapable of defeat—standing thus, cool and awakened, use the hearing you have acquired by pain and by the destruction of pain. Only fragments of the great song come to your ears while yet you are but man. But, if you listen to it, remember it faithfully, so that none which has reached you is lost, and endeavor to learn from it the meaning of the mystery which surrounds you. In time you will need no teacher. For as the individual has voice, so has that in which the individual exists. Life itself has speech and is never silent. And its utterance is not, as you that are deaf may suppose, a cry: it is a song. Learn from it that you are a part of the harmony; learn from it to obey the laws of the harmony.

"Listen to the song of life."

The note that is attached to this precept is so beautiful—so full of truth—so instructive—that we can find nothing to add to it, and we insert it in this place as the best possible explanation of the precept to which it is attached:

NOTE.—Look for it, and listen to it, first in your own heart. At first you may say it is not there; when I search I find only discord. Look deeper. If again you are disappointed, pause, and look deeper again. There is a natural melody, an obscure fount, in every human heart. It may be hidden over and utterly concealed and silenced—but it is there. At the very base of your nature, you will find faith, hope and love. He that chooses evil refuses to look within himself, shuts his ears to the melody of his heart, as he blinds his eyes to the light of his soul. He does this because he finds it easier to live in desires. But underneath all life is the strong current that cannot be checked; the great waters are there in reality. Find them, and you will perceive that none, not the most wretched of creatures, but is a part of it, however he blind himself to the fact, and build up for himself a phantasmal outer form of horror. In that sense it is that I say to you: All those beings among whom you struggle on are fragments of the Divine. And so deceptive is the illusion in which you live, that it is hard to guess where you will first detect the sweet voice in the hearts of others. But know that it is certainly within yourself. Look for it there and, once having heard it, you will more readily recognize it around you.

The sixth precept: "Store in your memory the melody you hear," and the seventh precept: "Learn from it the lesson of harmony," relate to the fifth precept and need no special explanation.

The eighth precept is full of information. It starts with the assurance that you (now being open to the guidance of Spirit) can stand upright, firm as a rock amid the turmoil, obeying the warrior (Spirit), who is spoken of as being "thyself and thy king" (again a reference to the relative and the absolute relation).

It speaks of the soul led by Spirit as being unconcerned in the battle, save to do his (Spirit's) bidding, and "having no longer any care as to the result of the battle" (that is, caring nothing about the apparent result—the temporary defeats, pains, and trying circumstances)—for only one thing is important and that is that Spirit should win, and win it must, for it is invincible, and incapable of defeat. The soul is spoken of as "standing thus, cool and awakened," and using the hearing which it has acquired by pain and by the destruction of pain. This paradox of "pain and the destruction of pain" is interesting. One necessarily learns lessons from pain—many lessons may be learned in no other way—and yet after the true nature of pain is learned and fully impressed upon the mind, then pain no longer is *pain*—pain is destroyed, and another lesson is learned. And so the voice of the Spirit—the song of life—comes to the hearing which has been awakened both by pain and by the destruction of pain.

"Only fragments of the great song come to your ears while you are but man." For when you reach the stage when you may listen to the grand volume of the divine song, then you are no longer man, but are something far higher in the scale of spiritual evolution and life. But the mere fragments of the song are so far beyond any other human experience that the mere echo is worth living a life to hear. We are further told that "if you listen to it, remember it faithfully, so that none which has reached you is lost, and endeavor to learn from it the meaning of the mystery which surrounds you," the voice of Spirit will beat upon your ears, so that, in spite of the material interferences you will from time to time have borne in upon your consciousness bits of knowledge which will seem to come from another world. Light will be thrown gradually upon the great problems of existence, and veil after veil will be withdrawn.

The precept then gives us the glad tidings that: "In time you will need no teacher. For as the individual has voice, so has that in which the individual

exists. Life has speech and is never silent. And it
is not, as you that are deaf may suppose, a cry; it is
a song. Learn from it that you are a part of the harmony; learn from it to obey the laws of the harmony."
In time you will have passed beyond the need of a
human teacher, for the light of Spirit will illuminate
every object upon which you gaze, and the ears opened
by Spirit will hear the lessons coming from every
object in nature. In the stone; in the plant; in the
mountain; in the tempest; in the sunshine; in the
stars; in all things high or low; will you perceive that
great throbbing intelligent life of which you are a part
—and from them will you hear notes of the great
song of life: "All is One; All is One." As the precept tells us, the sound from nature and nature's
things, is not a cry, as many have supposed, but a
great triumphant song—a song rejoicing in the flow
of life of the singer, and vibrating in unison with the
Absolute. "Learn from the song that you are a part
of the harmony; learn from it to obey the law of the
harmony."

The next group of four precepts are along the same
lines as those preceding:

9.   Regard earnestly all the life that surrounds you.
10.   Learn to look intelligently into the hearts of men.
11.   Regard most earnestly your own heart.
12.   For through your own heart comes the one light
which can illuminate life, and make it clear to your eyes.

Study the hearts of men, that you may know what is
that world in which you live, and of which you will to be
a part. Regard the constantly changing and moving life
which surrounds you, for it is formed by the hearts of men;
and, as you learn to understand their constitution and meaning, you will by degrees be able to read the larger word of
life.

The ninth precept: "Regard earnestly all the life that surrounds you," refers to that part of the subject mentioned by us in the preceding paragraph—the knowledge that comes to one by viewing nature by the light of the Spirit.

The tenth precept tells you to "Learn to look intelligently into the hearts of men, that you may understand the world of men, that forms a part of the great world. By knowing men you will be able to help them, and will also learn many lessons that will aid you in your journey along the path. But take notice of what the little accompanying note says regarding this study of men. Here it is:

Note.—From an absolutely impersonal point of view, otherwise your sight is colored. Therefore impersonality must first be understood.

Intelligence is impartial; no man is your enemy, no man is your friend. All alike are your teachers. Your enemy becomes a mystery that must be solved, even though it take ages; for man must be understood. Your friend becomes a part of yourself, an extension of yourself, a riddle hard to read. Only one thing is more difficult to know—your own heart. Not until the bonds of personality are loosed, can that profound mystery of self begin to be seen. Not until you stand aside from it, will it in any way reveal itself to your understanding. Then, and not till then, can you grasp and guide it. Then, and not till then, can you use all its powers, and devote them to a worthy service.

The eleventh precept tells you to "Regard most earnestly your own heart." And the twelfth precept goes on to say: "For through your own heart comes the one light which can illuminate life, and make it clear to your eyes." In your own nature you will find all that is in the nature of other men—high and low —pure and foul—it is all there, the foul outlived, per- haps—the pure yet to be lived, perhaps—but all there

And if you would understand men, and their motives. and their doings, and their thoughts, look within, and you will understand other men better. But do not identify yourself with all the thoughts you may find in your heart. View them as would an outsider, look at them as you would upon objects in a case in a museum—useful to study but not to make a part of your life. And, remember this, that *none* of the things in your heart is good enough to *use* or master you—although many of them may be *used by* you to *advantage.* YOU are the master, and not the mastered—that is if you are a delivered soul.

The thirteenth precept says that: "Speech comes only with knowledge. Attain to knowledge, and you will attain to speech." The little accompanying note is explanatory (in part) of this precept. We herewith print it:

NOTE.—It is impossible to help others till you have obtained some certainty of your own. When you have learned the first twenty-one rules, and have entered the Hall of Learning with your powers developed and sense unchained, then you will find there is a fount within you from which speech will arise.

Do not be worried if you anticipate being called upon to impart words of comfort and knowledge to others. You need not prepare yourself. The person will draw forth from you (through Spirit's guidance) just what is best for him or her. Fear not—have faith.

We must come to an end. We have tried to explain, partially, the wonderful teachings of this little manual—"*Light on the Path,*" so that the beginner, perhaps, might be able to grasp the loose end of the teaching, and then gradually unwind the ball at his leisure. The task has grown heavier, and the work less satisfactory, as the precepts passed before us. Words are finite—truth is infinite—and it is hard to even attempt to explain infinite truth in finite words. The thirteenth precept is the last one that we may consider. The remaining ones must be read alone by the student, with the light of the Spirit. They are only for those who have attained spiritual sight, and to such their meaning will be more or less plain, according to the degree of unfoldment which has come to the individual.

We feel that our task has been poorly executed, although many have written us that these lessons have opened their spiritual eyes, and that many things heretofore very dark, are now seen plainly. We trust that this is indeed so, and that many more may obtain help and comfort from our words, although to us it seems that we have written nothing. And yet, we know that if these words had not some task assigned to them—if they were not intended to form a part of the great work, they never would have been written. So we send them forth to go where they will, without a full knowledge on our part of their destination. Perhaps some into whose hands they may fall may understand better than do we why they were written and sent forth. They were produced at the dictates of Spirit—let Spirit attend to the placing of them where they are called for.

In our following lessons we will take up other phases of occultism which may be of interest and profit to our students. But before leaving the beautiful precepts and teachings of *"Light on the Path,"* let us urge upon our students the importance of that little manual. It contains within its pages the greatest amount of high spiritual teaching ever combined into so small a space. Let not the student imagine that he has mastered it, because he seems to understand its general teachings. Let him read it again a little later on, and he will see new beauties in it. We have never met a student—no matter how highly developed—who could not learn something from the little manual. Its teachings are capable of being interpreted in many different ways, for it portrays the experiences of the soul as it journeys along the path. You will remember that the upward ascent is along the spiral path, and the soul goes around and around but ever mounting higher. One may think he grasps the meaning of the first precepts of the little manual, but as he again reaches a certain point, just one round higher, he may again take up the first precepts and find in them new meaning suitable for his newly discovered needs. And so on, and so on. Not only is there spiritual progression along spiral lines extending over ages, but in each life-time there is a spiral path to be mounted, as will be apparent to all of us who will stop to consider the matter. The soul which has not found the entrance to the path, seems to go around and around in a circle, traveling over the same ground, and making no real progress. But once it discovers the little path which enters the circle at one of its points, and takes steps thereon, it finds that while it still goes around and around, it is really traveling the spiral, and is mounting one round higher with each turn. And we know of no little book so helpful on the journey as this little manual—"*Light on the Path.*"

We trust that we may be pardoned for inserting in this lesson the following words from our introduction to the little manual in question. They are as appropriate at the close of this lesson as at the beginning of the little book:

The treatise, "LIGHT ON THE PATH," is a classic among occultists, and is the best guide known for those who have taken the first step on the Path of Attainment. Its writer has veiled the meaning of the rules in the way always customary to mystics, so that to the one who has no grasp on the Truth these pages will probably appear to be a mass of contradictions and practically devoid of sense. But to the one to whom a glimpse of the inner life has been given, these pages will be a treasury of the rarest jewels, and each time he opens it he will see new gems. To many this little book will be the first revelation of that which they have been all their lives blindly seeking. To many it will be the first bit of spiritual bread given to satisfy the hunger of the soul. To many it will be the first cup of water from the spring of life, given to quench the thirst which has consumed them. Those for whom this book is intended will recognize its message, and after reading it they will never be the same as before it came to them. As the poet has said: "Where I pass all my children know me," and so will the Children of the Light recognize this book as for them. As for the others, we can only say that they will in time be ready for this great message. The book is intended to symbolize the successive steps of the neophyte in occultism as he progresses in the lodge work. The rules are practically those which were given to the neophytes in the great lodge of the Brotherhood in ancient Egypt, and which for generations have been taught by guru to chela in India. The peculiarity of the rules herein laid down, is that their inner meaning unfolds as the student progresses on The Path. Some will be able to understand a number of these rules, while others will see but dimly even the first steps. The student, however, will find that when he has firmly planted his foot on one of these steps, he will find the one just ahead becoming dimly illuminated, so as to give him confidence to take the next step. Let none be discouraged; the fact that this book attracts you is the message to you that it is intended for you, and will in time unfold its meaning. Read it over and over often, and you will find veil after veil lifted, though veil upon veil still remains between you and the Absolute.

This is the end of this publication.

Any remaining blank pages are for our book binding requirements and are blank on purpose.

To search thousands of interesting publications like this one, please remember to visit our website at:

http://www.kessinger.net

CPSIA information can be obtained
at www.ICGtesting.com
Printed in the USA
BVHW040410040720
582952BV00015B/1162

9 781162 870205